THIS WALKER BOOK BELONGS TO:

Geraldine King

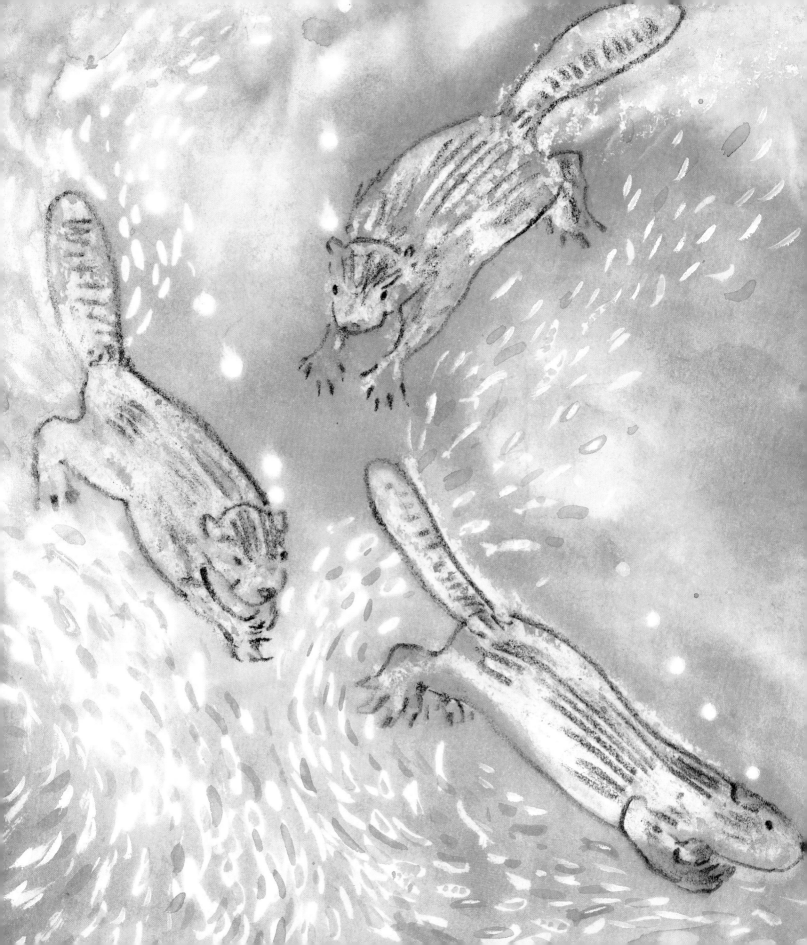

On land,
beavers move quite
clumsily, but in the water
they are swift, streamlined
and graceful. A special membrane
protects their eyes while they're
swimming, so they can
see under water, too.

For Willie Llewellyn
K.W.

For Lotte Manning
M.M.

First published 1993
by Walker Books Ltd
87 Vauxhall Walk
London SE11 5HJ

This edition published 2001

10 9 8 7 6 5 4 3 2 1

Text © 1993 Karen Wallace
Illustrations © 1993 Mick Manning

Printed in Hong Kong

British Library Cataloguing
in Publication Data:
a catalogue record for
this book is available
from the British Library

ISBN 0-7445-8222-9

# THINK of a BEAVER

Karen Wallace

illustrated by
Mick Manning

WALKER BOOKS
AND SUBSIDIARIES
LONDON • BOSTON • SYDNEY

Think of a beaver.

The beavers in this book live in North America, but there are beavers in Europe and Asia as well.

Bright-eyed beaver, brown and bushy,

hurries to the stony lake shore.

Beavers dam the stream with sticks, stones, roots and mud to make a pond.

Beaver breath is hot and woody –

he's grunting, puffing, dragging branches.

Beaver teeth

are sharp as chisels,

orange like

an autumn pumpkin.

Beaver teeth

can cut through trees,

and grow again

when beaver breaks them.

*Beavers eat lily roots.
They also eat bark and
young wood from aspen
and birch trees.*

Beaver hands
are monkey clever.
He builds a lodge
from mud and branches,
tunnels in
from under water.

Beavers usually build their
lodge in the middle of the
pond. They leave spaces
in the roof to let in air.

Most beaver lodges have at least two tunnels.

A beaver can swim for a quarter of a mile without coming up for air.

Beaver feet are webbed
like ducks' feet,
push like paddles
through the water,
past the slowly
swimming salmon,
down to where
the tangled roots
lie buried in
the reedy lake bed.

*Beaver feet are useful
for grooming, too.*

Beavers live in families. Couples mate for life.

Beaver tail
is flat and scaly,
like a rudder
under water,
like a trowel
for mud and branches,
carefully curled
and carried safely.

Beaver tail
sounds danger warning.
He whacks it SLAP!
upon the water.
Other beavers
hear the message…

Quickly dive!

Protect the young ones!

Find the tunnel

under water!

19

Baby beavers are called kits.
A mother beaver usually
has two to four kits at a time.

Beaver kits are born
in May-time,
dry and warm
on wood-chip bedding.

They cry like children
when they're hungry.

They learn to swim
along the tunnel,
through the water
to the lodge roof.

They play like children
in the sunshine.

Brainy beaver, engineer now,

cuts canals through boggy meadows.

He chooses trees beyond the shore,

chops them down and floats them home.

Beaver couples work together.

When the days
are growing colder,
leaves are falling,
red and yellow,
busy beaver's
work is hardest.

He gathers wood
for winter eating,
for when the ice
is hard as iron.

He plasters mud
and sticks together,
mends his dam,
protects his shelter
against the cold
and snowy weather.

*Beavers greet each other
by chattering...*

*and nibbling each
other's cheeks.*

Bushy beaver's
warm in winter.
He doesn't mind
the icy water.

He grows two coats
to keep the cold out –
thick and silky
on the skin side,
rough and rainproof
on the outside.

All winter long,

while snow is falling,

when birds have flown

and bears are sleeping,

beaver lives

inside his lodge room,

warm and dry

on wood-chip bedding.

He nibbles at

his sunken branches,

combs his fur

and waits for spring.

Think of a beaver.

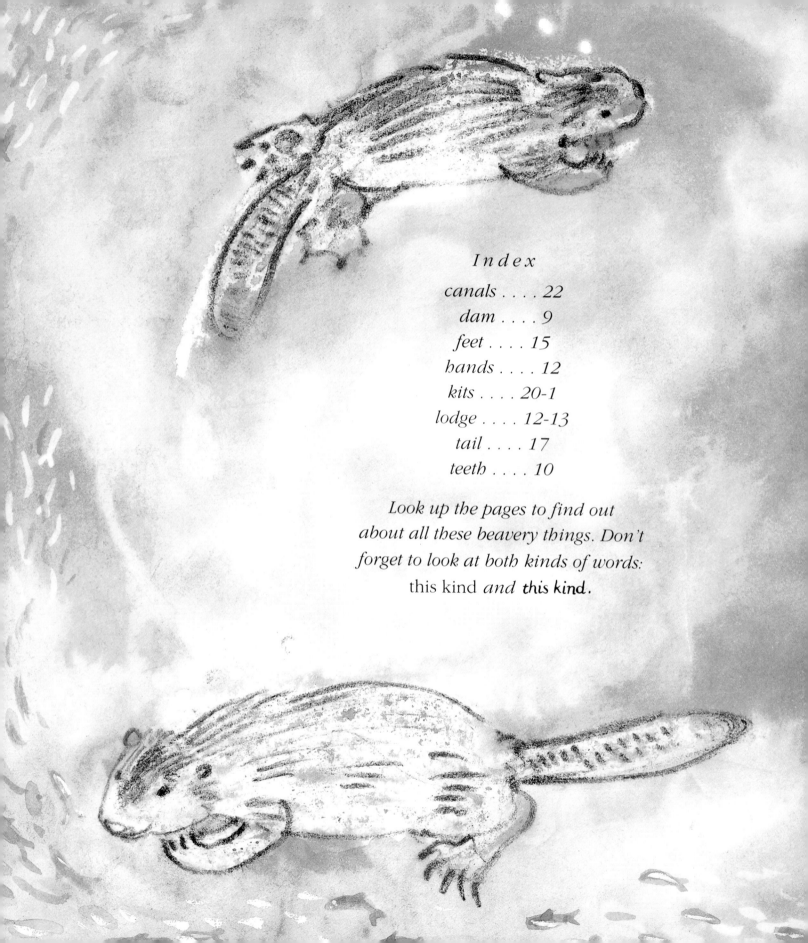

*Look up the pages to find out about all these beavery things. Don't forget to look at both kinds of words:* this kind *and* **this kind.**

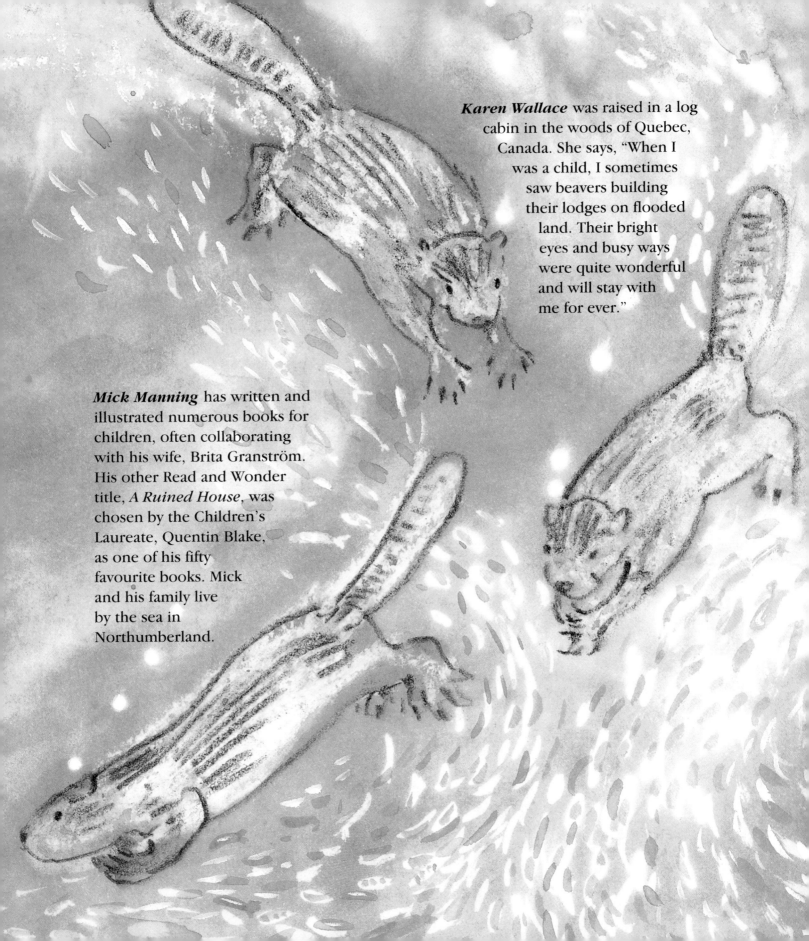

**Karen Wallace** was raised in a log cabin in the woods of Quebec, Canada. She says, "When I was a child, I sometimes saw beavers building their lodges on flooded land. Their bright eyes and busy ways were quite wonderful and will stay with me for ever."

**Mick Manning** has written and illustrated numerous books for children, often collaborating with his wife, Brita Granström. His other Read and Wonder title, *A Ruined House*, was chosen by the Children's Laureate, Quentin Blake, as one of his fifty favourite books. Mick and his family live by the sea in Northumberland.

# NOTES FOR TEACHERS

The READ AND WONDER series is an innovative and versatile resource for reading, thinking and discovery. Each book invites children to become excited about a topic, see how varied information books can be, and want to find out more.

☞ **Reading aloud** The story form makes these books ideal for reading aloud – in their own right or as part of a cross-curricular topic, to a child or to a whole class. After you've introduced children to the books in this way, they can revisit and enjoy them again and again.

☞ **Shared reading** Big Book editions are available for several titles, so children can read along, discuss the topic, and comment on the different ways information is presented – to wonder together.

☞ **Group and guided reading** Children need to experience a range of reading materials. Information books like these help develop the skills of reading to learn, as part of learning to read. With the support of a reading group, children can become confident, flexible readers.

☞ **Paired reading** It's fun to take turns to read the information in the main text or captions. With a partner, children can explore the pages to satisfy their curiosity and build their understanding.

☞ **Individual reading** These books can be read for interest and pleasure by children at home and in school.

☞ **Research** Once children have been introduced to these books through reading aloud, they can use them for independent or group research, as part of a curricular topic.

☞ **Children's own writing** You can offer these books as strong models for children's own information writing. They can record their observations and findings about a topic, make field notes and sketches, and add extra snippets of information for the reader.

Above all, Read and Wonders are to be enjoyed, and encourage children to develop a lasting curiosity about the world they live in.

*Sue Ellis, Centre for Language in Primary Education*